People of Scotland 1

Dorothy Morrison

Oliver & Boyd

Introduction

The stories in this book are about people who lived long ago. Their lives are part of the history of Scotland. Perhaps some of them lived near where you stay. Every place has a history made by the people who lived there. Your mother and father have helped to make yesterday's history. What you do will become part of history too. You are part of the story of the people of Scotland.

Teacher's Note

Most of these stories were well known to earlier generations of Scottish children. They still deserve to be told today for they introduce some of the main features of the history of Scotland. The early church, the struggle for Independence, medieval life, renaissance ideas, the Stewart monarchs, superstition, religious conflict, the clan system and the Jacobite risings are all presented in a very simple way through stories. The enjoyment of a good story can stimulate a lasting interest in history which can be more fully developed in later studies of the national environment. Stories from various parts of the country have been included to show the wide variety of incident and location which is part of the story of the people of Scotland.

Contents

1. The Fish and the Ring

Long ago Roderick was King of Strathclyde. He gave his wife a very fine gold ring. She wore it every day and everyone admired it.

One day the King was away on a visit, and the Queen wished to give a gift to one of the nobles. She looked at her fine gold ring. "Perhaps this ring will do," she said.

She took the ring from her finger and gave it to the noble.

He was very pleased. He tried the ring on his middle finger. It did not fit. Then he tried the second finger. The ring was just too small, so he put it on his little finger.

As he rode along the banks of the River Clyde, he met a friend. He waved his hand to greet him. The ring flew off and fell in the deep water!

Two days later the King came home. When he saw that his wife was not wearing the ring, he said, "Go and put on your fine gold ring!"

The Queen did not know what to do. She was afraid her husband would be very angry. She had heard about a man called Mungo who lived nearby. People said he could do wonderful things.

She sent for Mungo, and told him her problem.

"Please help me," she said.

Mungo went with the Queen to the edge of the river. A fisherman was watching. "Cast your net here," Mungo ordered.

The man pulled in his net. Inside was a large salmon. When the fish was cut open, the Queen's ring was inside!

People were amazed. "Mungo must be a saint!" they said.

The Fish and the Ring

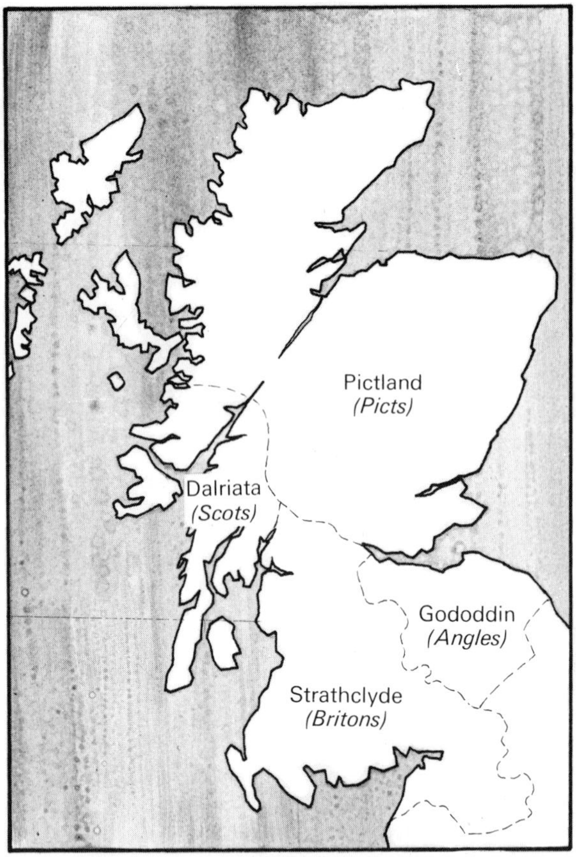

Scotland was not always one country. It was made up of four peoples. They came from different places. They did not speak the same language. They each had their own kings.

The map shows Strathclyde and the other kingdoms.

They made war and took land, weapons and food. Sometimes they made people slaves.

The Preachers

One thing helped to join them into one country. Men came to Scotland to teach the people about Jesus Christ. They built churches. People in each of the four kingdoms came to have the same God.

It was very hard to travel about Scotland to preach. There were wolves, bears, wild cats and boars in the forests.

At first people tried to kill the preachers. These brave men lived such good lives that soon they were called saints.

St Ninian

The first preacher who came to Scotland was St Ninian. He set up the first church in Scotland at Whithorn 1500 years ago. It was only a small white hut.

When St Ninian died other men like St Mungo carried on his work. St Mungo built a church of wood and clay near Glasgow. It was not very big but it stood on a hilltop above the river. People came for miles to hear him preach. It was said that his mother was a princess. There were stories told that he could work miracles.

Other Saints

Perhaps you know of some of these saints:
St Serf, St Drostan, St Cuthbert, St Enoch, St Columba.

St Mungo is the patron saint of Glasgow. The motto of the city is: "Let Glasgow flourish (do well) by the preaching of the word." The coat of arms of Glasgow shows some of the stories told about St Mungo.

You can see a bird on a tree, a bell and a fish with a ring.

2. A Day's Fishing

One fine spring morning William Wallace went fishing in the river Irvine. Soon he had caught six fine trout.

"This is a lucky day for me," he thought. The boy with him put the trout in a basket to take home.

Just then two men came past. William looked up and scowled. He did not like them. They were English soldiers who had invaded Scotland.

"Just the thing for breakfast!" laughed one of the men. He grabbed hold of the basket.

"Stop!" cried William. "You can have half the fish. Don't take the whole basket."

The soldiers would not listen. One of them drew his sword.

William was so angry that he did not think what he was doing. He used the heavy end of his fishing rod to hit the man on the head. To his surprise and horror, the man fell dead.

Before the other soldier could turn on him, he picked up the dead man's sword. He fought bravely and the second soldier soon ran off.

William had saved his fish but now he was in danger. The leader of the English soldiers would be sure to hunt him down. The only thing to do was to leave home and hide out in the hills.

It had not been such a lucky day after all!

A Day's Fishing

William Wallace is a great Scottish hero. There is a monument to Wallace at Stirling. At Edinburgh Castle there is a statue of Wallace.

The Hammer of the Scots

When Wallace was a boy, the King of England was Edward I. He wanted to rule Scotland as well. Then he would have one big, strong country. He took an army to Scotland and put English soldiers in the castles. People called Edward "the Hammer of the Scots".

Wallace against the English

When Wallace grew up, he led an army to drive the English out of Scotland. Many Scots helped him. He won a great victory at Stirling Bridge.
Later a man helped English soldiers to capture Wallace. He was taken to England and put to death.

Edward's Army

In the army Edward I brought to Scotland there were archers and spearmen and knights. The knights wore armour and rode very strong horses.

In the picture you can see how a knight was dressed.
He had a helmet to protect his head.
On his body he wore chain mail. It was made of iron rings linked together. He carried a wooden shield, a sword and an axe.

3. The King and the Old Woman

Robert Bruce was tired and hungry. His armour was heavy and he had walked many miles.

That morning five men had attacked him. He had been lucky to escape but the faithful servant with him had been killed. Now he was alone. His enemies were hunting all over Galloway for him. They did not want him to rule Scotland.

At last he came to a small cottage. When he knocked at the door an old woman opened it.

"Who are you?" she asked. "What do you want?"

"I am a traveller," said Bruce. "Can you give me some food and let me rest for a while?"

"All travellers are welcome in my house, for the sake of one," replied the old woman. "Come in."

"Who is the traveller you speak of?" asked Bruce as he sat by the fire.

The old lady looked at him.

"It is the king, Robert Bruce," she said. "He is hunted by the English and their friends. I know he is the king who should rule the Scots. If he comes here I will welcome him gladly."

Robert Bruce stood up. "I am the king," he said.

The old woman was amazed. "Why are you all alone, Your Majesty? Where are all your men?" she asked. Bruce told her what had happened.

"You must have men to guard you," said the old woman. "I have two strong sons. They will be proud to fight for you."

She opened the door and called out, "Willie! John! Come here! Your king has need of you!"

Two tall strong men came running up. When they saw the king they knelt down. They gave a promise to serve him all their lives.

Their mother smiled happily. Then she turned to stir the pot hanging over the fire. She wanted to give the king a good supper.

All at once there was a loud noise. Many men on horseback were outside.

"Fight for your king!" cried the old woman to her sons.

Armed men pushed open the door of the cottage. Bruce stood with his sword drawn. Then he laughed.

Do not fear, old woman," he said. "Your sons need not fight today. This is my brother and the good Lord James. See, they have brought an army to help me! But I'll never forget that when I was alone you gave me your two fine sons. They will always be my friends!"

The King and the Old Woman

After William Wallace died, the Scots still tried to put the English out of Scotland. In 1306 Robert Bruce was crowned King of Scots.
At first things went badly. He lost a battle with the English. There was no safe place where he could stay. He was not sure whether he should carry on fighting.

Bruce and the Spider

Many stories are told about Bruce at this time. Perhaps you know the famous story about Bruce and the spider.

Bruce was hiding in a cave. He saw a spider trying to spin its web from one side to the other. Time after time it tried but could not reach the other side. It did not give up. At last when it tried for the tenth time its web went right across the cave. Bruce thought this was a good sign. He made up his mind to keep trying to make Scotland free. He was sure that one day, just like the spider, he would win.

**If at first you don't succeed
try, try, try again.**

Bannockburn

He was right. He kept on fighting. More people joined his army. He took castles from the English. At last in 1314 he won a great victory at Bannockburn. In the end, the English agreed that they should not rule Scotland.

An old poem tells what Bruce said to his men at Bannockburn:

> "... we, for our lives
> and for our children and our wives
> and for the freedom of our land
> are bound in battle for to stand."

4. The Capture of the Castle

Farmer Binnock smiled to the English soldier.

"Tell your leader I will deliver the hay he wants tomorrow," he said.

As the soldier went off back to Linlithgow Palace, Binnock laughed. "I will take more than hay to the castle," he told his servant Jock. "I have a plan to help King Robert Bruce drive out the English."

"But the castle is full of armed men," said Jock. "Even if you could get through the gate, you could not pass the portcullis. When they let it down the big iron spikes at the bottom would crash on top of you."

Binnock told Jock what he planned to do.

That night he gathered all the men who lived nearby. While it was dark they crept up to the walls of the castle and hid.

"Remember," said Binnock in a whisper, "do not move until you hear me shout 'Call all!.' "

Early next morning Jock drove a huge heavy cart piled high with hay to the castle. Underneath the hay eight strong armed men lay hidden.

The watchman saw the cart with Binnock walking beside it. He hurried to open the gate.

As the cart rumbled through the gateway, Jock leaned forward. He cut the harness which held the horses to the cart. They galloped off into the courtyard, leaving the cart behind.

Binnock shouted, "Call all! Call all!" Out jumped the men from the cart. Quickly the English soldiers dropped the portcullis. Because of the cart it could not touch the ground. Binnock's men were able to rush in from outside.

The soldiers in the castle were taken by surprise. In no time they were prisoners.

Binnock had captured the castle!

The Capture of the Castle

King Robert Bruce had to win back all the castles in Scotland from the English. These pictures show how hard it would be to attack a castle.

Sometimes castles were built on high rocks. From inside you could see enemies coming while they were still far away. To get into a castle like this one you had to climb the rock.

Other castles had a deep ditch round about. Sometimes it was filled with water. A drawbridge was let down from the castle. This let people go in and out. When enemies came the drawbridge could be pulled up.

Behind the drawbridge there was a big, heavy gate. Behind the gate was the portcullis made of iron. It had sharp spikes at the bottom. At a time of danger the portcullis could fall quickly. You can see that Farmer Binnock's idea was a clever trick. Here are some other ways to attack a castle.

Use a battering ram.

Build a wooden tower outside.

Mine under the castle.

5. Murder of the King!

King James and Queen Joanna sat by the fire. The queen's ladies-in-waiting were with them.

There was a knock at the door. An old Highland woman was asking to see the king. She wished to warn him of danger.

"It is much too late to bother His Majesty with such nonsense," said one of the ladies. "Tell her to come back tomorrow."

Just then a sudden gleam of light could be seen at the window. Armed men carrying torches were in the garden!

"My enemies have come to kill me!" cried the king. "Quickly! Bar the door and give me time to escape."

The windows were fastened tightly and could not be opened. There was only one thing to do. The king snatched up the tongs at the fireside and raised up a plank in the floor. Underneath was a small, narrow tunnel which led to the courtyard. Hastily he let himself down and the plank was closed over the top. Then he remembered that he had ordered the tunnel to be blocked up, because his tennis balls sometimes rolled into the hole.

The king was trapped!

In the room above Queen Joanna and her ladies tried to keep the door shut. Someone had taken away the bar which was used to close the door at night. Bravely Catherine Douglas put her own arm into the place for the bar. As the plotters pushed against the door her arm broke. She fainted with pain. Men armed with swords and daggers rushed in, pushing the women roughly aside.

"Where is the king?" they shouted.

The queen stood on top of the hatch leading to the tunnel. The plotters thought the king must have escaped. When they went out to search other rooms, the ladies hurried to help the king.

At this unlucky moment the traitors came back. One after another they jumped down to attack the king who had no weapons to defend himself. He fought bravely but fell covered in stab wounds.

The king's servants and the people of the town came hurrying to the rescue, but it was too late. The King of Scotland lay dead.

Murder of the King

King James I of Scotland tried to be a good king. He made wise laws which were fair to everyone. To rule well he needed money to run the country. People had to pay taxes. Because he was very strict and made everyone obey his laws, some barons did not like him. They made a plot to kill him.

Some Laws made by James

People must practise with bows and arrows so that they can use them well.

Everyone who has land must kill young crows to stop them eating the crops.

Every baron must hunt for wolves in his lands four times a year.

Very poor people will be allowed to beg.

Poor people in trouble with the law can get free help.

Every man over 16 must keep weapons to fight with in war-time.

People must not waste time playing football or golf.

Where James I died

King James spent his Christmas holiday at Perth. He stayed in a monastery with the Black Friars. It was not as strong as a castle. There was not enough room for all his men. It was easy for his enemies to get in to kill him.

After James died

When James I died his son became the new king. He was only six years old. He could not rule the country by himself. People were very sad they had lost such a good king as James.

Lady Catherine Douglas had tried to save the king. People called her Kate Barlass.

6. Damian Tries to Fly

Damian woke early that morning in Stirling Castle. He rushed to the window of his room in the turret and looked out. It was raining and a strong wind blew from the north.

"Good," he thought. "If the weather is bad, I need not test the wings today. Of course, I know I can fly like a bird. Still, it is better if I wait a little longer."

After a short time the rain stopped and the sun came out. One of the king's men knocked on Damian's door.

"It is a fine day," he said. "Everything is ready, and the king is waiting."

Slowly Damian made his way to the high wall of the castle. He could see a great crowd standing at the foot of the rock far below.

Turning to King James he said, "Perhaps it is a little windy, Your Majesty. Shall I wait until tomorrow?"

"No," said the king firmly.

He always liked to try out new ideas. He was looking forward to seeing a man fly for the first time.

"You said you would fly from the top of the castle. Everything is ready. Look! Even the birds are waiting to see you!"

With a sad little smile Damian stretched out his arms. The heavy leather wings covered with feathers were strapped on. Two of the king's men pushed him forward. He looked down again. The ground seemed a very long way below.

He shut his eyes and took a deep breath. Then he jumped from the wall and flapped his arms.

The birds soared above him calling loudly. The wind rushed past him as he fell down ... down ... down. The more he flapped, the faster he seemed to fall. With a great thud he landed in a huge patch of mud at the foot of the castle. As he crawled out wet and muddy, everyone laughed.

"How stupid!" they said. "Men will never be able to fly!"

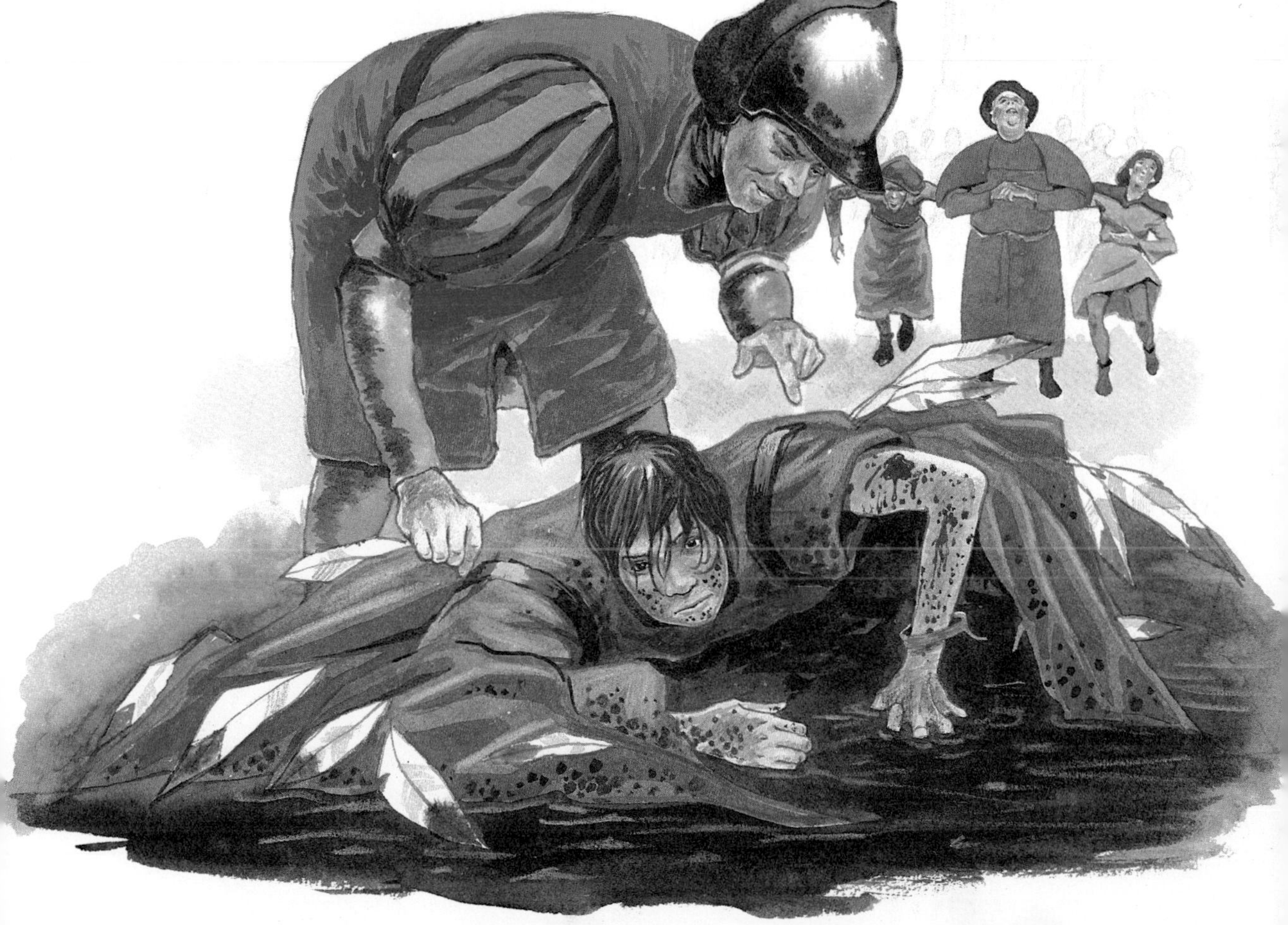

Damian Tries to Fly

Damian was lucky that he only broke a leg when he tried to fly. He told the king that he had been wrong to use hens' feathers for wings. Hens like to stay on the ground. He was sure that if he had used skylarks' feathers he would have been able to soar up into the sky.

Here is part of an old poem about Damian.

The birds that saw him in the sky
Began to wonder what he was
Free from his home-made wings he fell
And in a marsh, up to his eyes
Among the mud he slid.

There were no aeroplanes long ago. Men who wanted to fly watched the birds carefully. They saw birds flap their wings. Like Damian, they thought the best idea was to make wings for themselves. Then, if they jumped from a high place and flapped the wings quickly, they would be able to fly.

No one ever managed to fly this way. People are too heavy to fly like birds. Their arms are not strong enough.

Successful Fliers

The first men to fly used a huge balloon. It was filled with hot air. Because the hot air was very light, the balloon rose up into the sky.

Some men tried to fly with wings like a kite. The wings did not move. They were able to glide in the air.

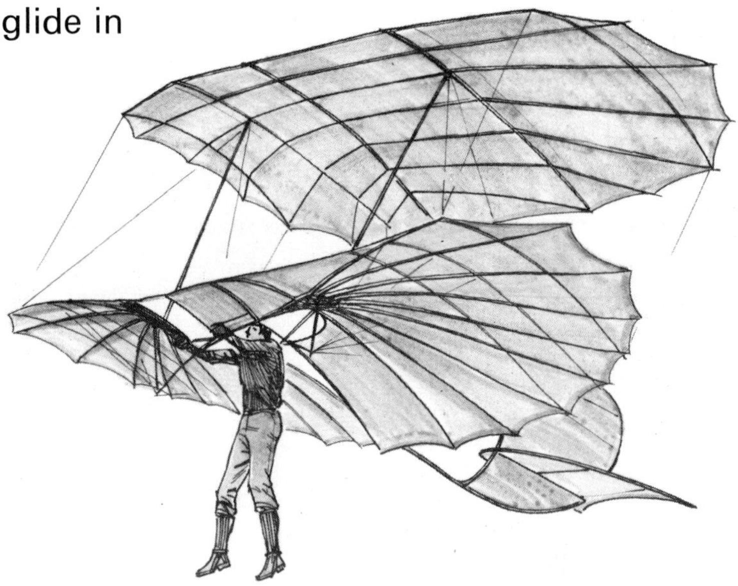

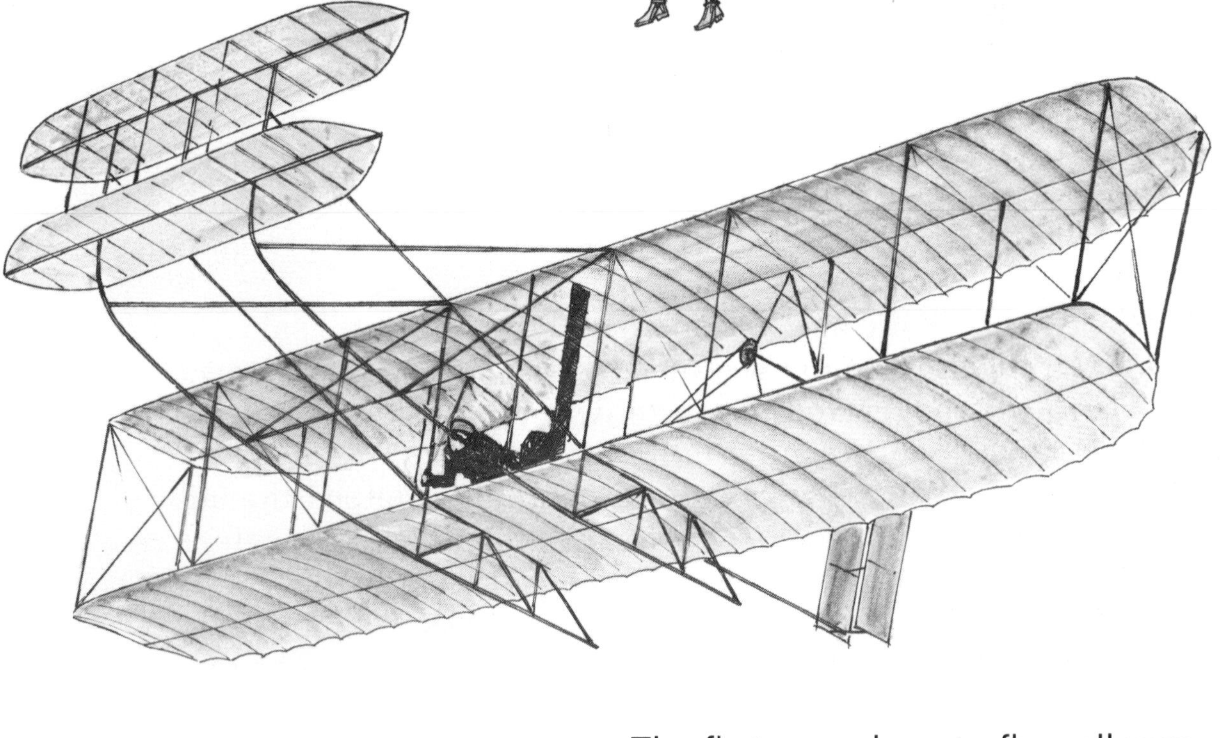

The first aeroplane to fly well was made by two brothers. Their names were Wilbur and Orville Wright. This was in 1903, nearly 400 years after Damian tried to fly. Their plane was called a biplane.

7. A Surprise for John

All morning John had worked hard threshing corn in the barn. Suddenly he heard noisy shouting and he rushed outside. On the tall narrow bridge of Cramond stood a man with his sword drawn. Four armed robbers were attacking him.

"Four against one is not a fair fight," said John. He jumped on to the bridge beside the stranger and began to beat the attackers with his heavy threshing flail.

When the robbers ran off, John helped the man into the barn. He brought him a basin of water and a towel to wash the blood from his face and hands. Then, to make sure that the robbers did not attack again, he walked part of the way to Edinburgh with him.

The stranger thanked John for his help and asked his name.

"John Howitson. I work at Braehead. It is one of the king's farms."

"My name is James of Ballengiech," said the stranger. "I have a simple job at the king's palace in Edinburgh. I would like to pay you back for all your kindness. Why not visit me next Sunday and I'll show you where the king stays?"

Next Sunday John put on his best clothes and bonnet when he went to visit. James of Ballengiech was waiting for him at a side door of the palace. He took him round all the grand empty rooms. John was only a poor labourer and he had never seen such fine wall hangings or chairs and tables so richly carved. When James asked if he would like to see the king and his nobles, John was thrilled.

"That would be wonderful," he said, "but tell me how I will know which man is the King?"

"That's easy," James told him as he opened a door. "Only the king will be wearing a hat."

John found himself in a great hall full of men richly dressed in velvet and lace. He felt very out of place in his rough woollen trousers and coarse linen shirt.

"I don't see the king," whispered John as he looked round. "We two are the only people wearing hats."

"That's right," laughed James. "You are the only man wearing a hat except the king!"

"Oh, Your Majesty!" cried John, bending low. "What a surprise! All this time I have been speaking to the king!"

A Surprise for John

1. When people grew corn long ago they cut it with a sickle.

2. Then they beat the grain from the stalks of corn with a heavy flail. It was made in two pieces so that it bent in the middle. No wonder the robbers ran off when John chased them with his flail.

3. Later the corn was taken to the mill to be ground into flour.

James V

King James V sometimes liked to dress as a poor man. He would pretend he had just a small piece of land. Then he could go about his kingdom freely. People did not know he was the king. He could find out things that were wrong and try to help.

He was lucky that John was there to help him when the robbers attacked. To show how pleased he was, the king gave John the farm on which he worked. He must do only one thing. Every time the king passed that way John must bring a basin and towel so that the king could wash his hands. John's family who came after him kept the farm in return for doing this too.

The King's Palace

The palace in Edinburgh is Holyroodhouse. It was more comfortable for James V to live there than in Edinburgh Castle a mile away. The Queen still stays in the palace when she visits Edinburgh.

The road from the palace to the castle is called the Royal Mile.

8. Escape from the Castle on the Island

Young Willie Douglas watched Mary Queen of Scots from a corner of the room. Mary looked sadly out of the window of the castle. Only a year ago she had been the ruler of Scotland, but now she was a prisoner on an island in the middle of Loch Leven. There was no chance of escape, as the keeper was very strict.

"I wish I could help her but I am only a page," Willie thought. "She is so beautiful. I do not believe the unkind things people say about her."

Willie began to work out a plan. By Sunday all was ready.

The keeper and his family were at supper. Very quietly Willie sneaked into the keeper's room. The big bunch of keys which opened all the doors of the castle lay on the table near the fire. He picked them up slowly in case anyone might hear a noise. Then he hurried up to the tower where the queen was kept a prisoner.

"Quick, Your Majesty!" he cried as he shone a light from the window. "Follow me! Your friends are waiting for you."

The queen and her lady-in-waiting wrapped themselves in warm clothes and crept downstairs. Willie locked the door of the great hall where everyone was at supper. Now no one could follow them.

He had a small boat waiting on the shore. Once the queen and her lady-in-waiting were safe on board, he rowed quickly across the loch.

Half way over he tossed the keys of the castle into the water.

"They won't find those keys easily," laughed Queen Mary.

As they reached land, men hurried forward to help her. They were happy that the queen was safe.

Before she rode off to Hamilton, the queen turned to Willie. She had tears in her eyes as she smiled at him.

"I will never forget that you set free the Queen of Scots," she said.

Escape from the Castle on the Island

Mary had a sad life. When she was only a baby, her father died. She became Queen of Scots. The English king tried to invade Scotland so she was sent to France to be safe. She did not come back to Scotland until she was nineteen.

Scotland had changed while she was away. Now many people did not like the church to which Mary belonged.

Mary and her husband Lord Darnley were not happy together. When he was killed, some people blamed Mary.

From One Prison to Another

Nobles fought against Mary and her new husband. Mary was made a prisoner and put in Loch Leven Castle. She was made to give up being queen. Her baby son, James, became the new king. When Willie Douglas helped Mary to escape she got a new army to help her. At the Battle of Langside her army lost. Mary did not know what to do. She fled to England and asked her cousin, Queen Elizabeth, to help her.

Mary's Death

Elizabeth put Mary in prison. Friends made plans to free her but they could not do it.

At last, after nineteen years, Queen Elizabeth gave orders to put Mary to death. In 1587 her head was cut off at Fotheringhay Castle. The sad queen's life had ended.

9. The Girl whose Mouth was too Big

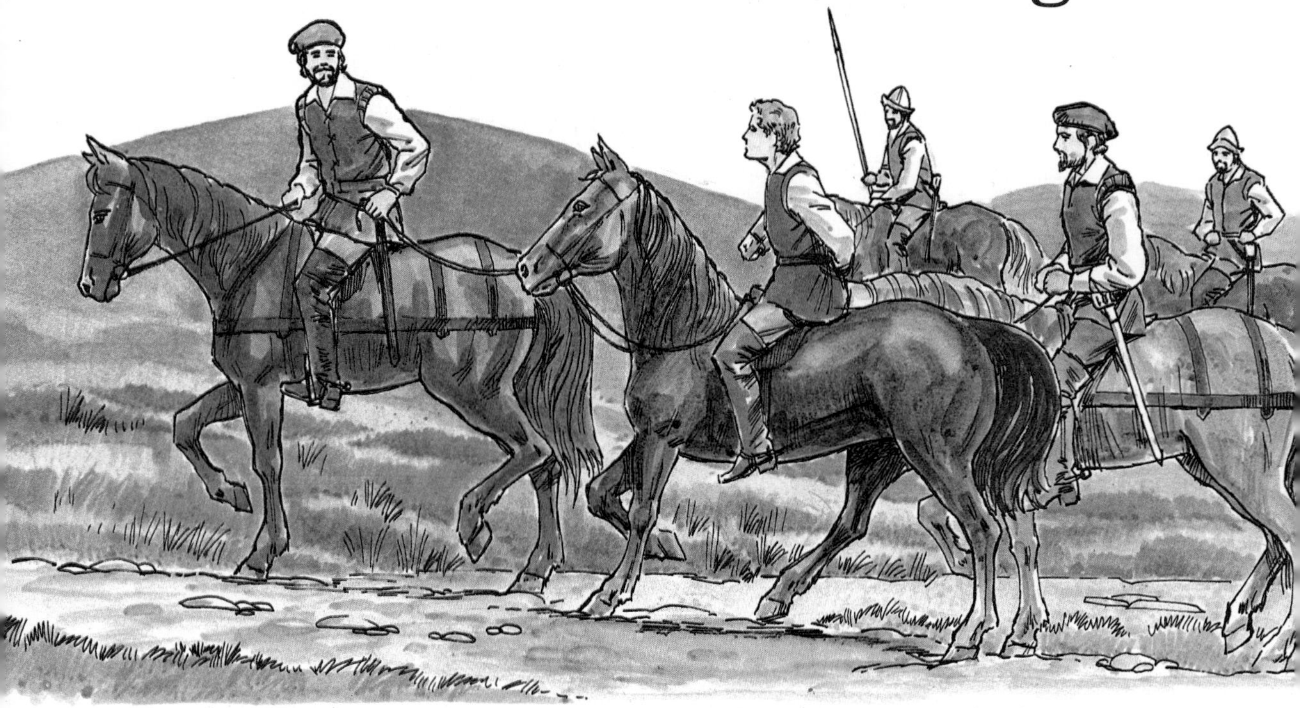

Things had gone well for young William Scott and his men. They had been on a raid in the lands of Sir Gideon Murray, Laird of Elibank. They were on their way home with all the goods they had stolen, when Sir Gideon and his men fell upon them. William Scott was captured and brought back to the castle of Elibank.

William was a good-looking young fellow. All the ladies of the castle crowded to the windows to look at him as he rode by.

"What will father do with him?" said Meg Murray sadly to her mother. "Will he put him to death? He is too fine a young man to die so young."

The Laird's wife looked at her youngest daughter. Her other daughters were well-known for their beauty. But Meg's mouth was so large that everyone joked about it. She was called "the lass with the muckle mouth". She was a kind, pleasant girl, but no man would ask her to marry him.

Meg's mother had an idea. She hurried off to speak to her husband.

"I will hang this young rogue," he said.

"I have a better plan," said his wife. "If you kill him, his family will attack us again. The fighting will go on and on. Let him choose. Tell him he will be hanged tomorrow unless he marries Meg. We will not give him any money or lands as her dowry."

William was not too keen to have Meg as his bride, but he agreed at last and a great wedding feast was held in the castle.

Meg was very pleased to have such a fine handsome husband. Although William had been forced to marry her, he found that she was a good, kind and loving wife. They lived happily together for the rest of their lives.

The Girl whose Mouth was too Big

The land where the countries of Scotland and England meet is called the Borders. At one time the people who lived there were very fond of fighting. They often crossed the border between the two countries to attack those on the other side. Sometimes they even attacked the people of their own country and took away their cattle and belongings.

Many of the people who lived in the Borders were very poor. Their lands were spoiled because men were always fighting each other.

Farms and houses were burnt. Crops in the fields were trampled by horses. Cattle were stolen. People were killed.

Revenge

If a man was put to death, his friends would try to get revenge. They did this even if the man had done wicked or evil things.

Meg's mother knew that if William Scott was hanged, his family would attack. Her idea was a good one. No one would harm the family of his bride.

Dowries

When a girl got married her father gave a present to her new husband. This was called a dowry. If the girl's father was rich, he would give land or money or jewels.

Meg's father gave no dowry when she married. William Scott still had a good bargain. His life had been saved!

10. The Baby in the Cave

The Laird of Invernahyle was a peaceful man. He wanted to stay friendly with everyone and had no wish to go to war. Most other men who lived in the Highlands of Scotland at that time loved to hunt and fight.

Nearby lived another laird called Green Colin. One spring day Colin and his men came marching up to attack Invernahyle. The laird and his family were taken by surprise. They had no chance to fight. Everyone in the house was killed and the house was set on fire.

The laird's baby son, Donald, was not at home. His nurse had been walking with him close by. When she saw what had happened, she hid the baby in a small cave in the rocks. She knew it would be hard to look after him so she tied a big piece of lard on a string round his neck. She hoped the baby would suck the lard and keep quiet so that no one would find him.

Green Colin's men searched everywhere for the baby. They did not want any of the laird's family left alive. When they found the nurse they kept her in prison for three days.

The nurse was sure that little Donald would be dead by that time.

"If he does not die of cold or hunger, then wolves or wild cats will eat him," she thought.

As soon as she was free, she hurried back to the cave. How happy she was to hear a faint cry! The baby lay where she had left him. There was only a little piece of lard the size of a nut on the string. Donald had sucked the rest.

The baby's nurse took him away to her own people of the MacDonald clan. She married a blacksmith and Donald was brought up as their son. He grew big and strong. Because he helped the blacksmith, everyone called him Donald of the Hammer.

When he was twenty-one, the smith told him how he had been rescued as a baby. With the six sons of the smith he gathered an army and went back to Invernahyle. Green Colin was killed in battle and Donald took back his father's lands again.

The baby in the cave had come home!

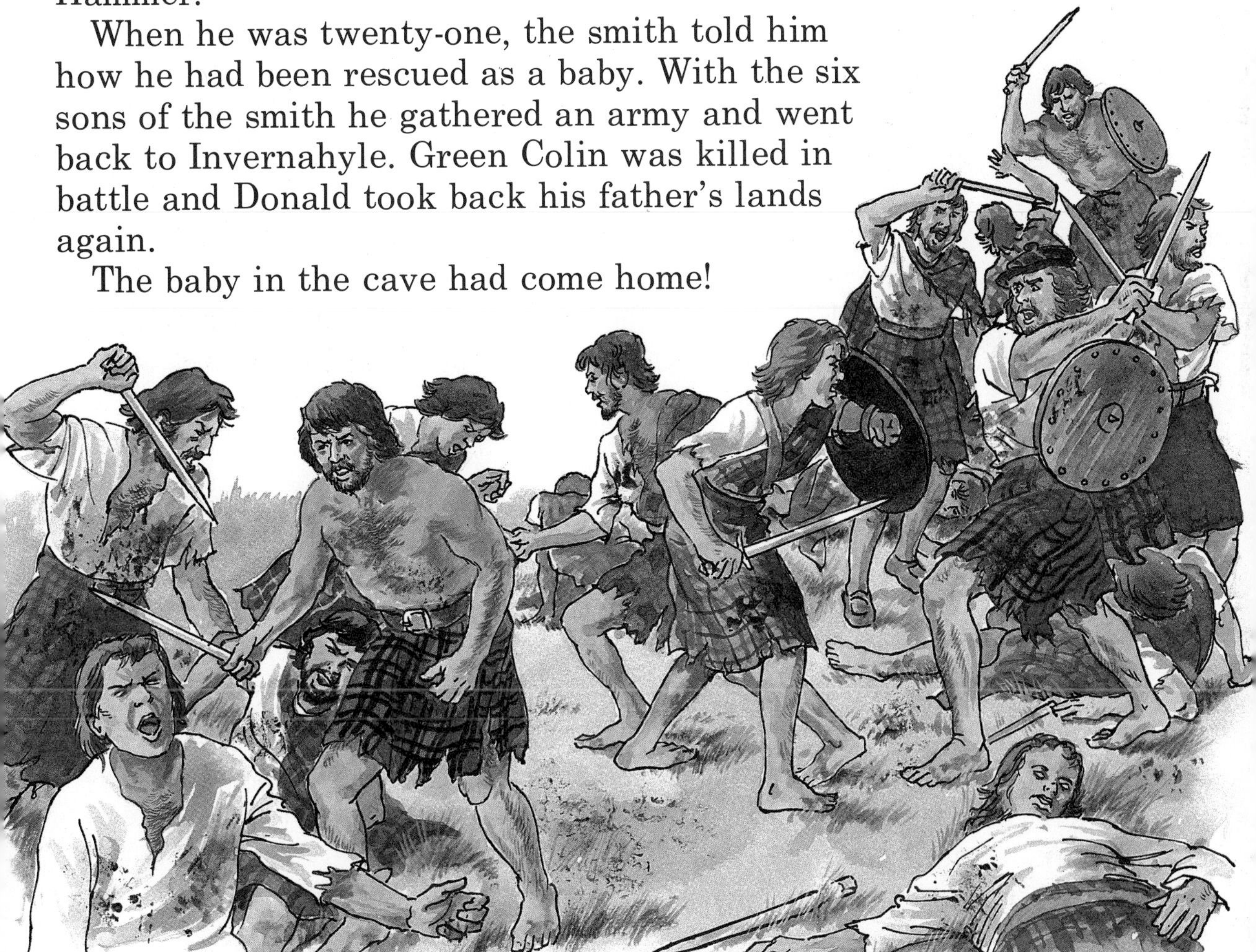

The Baby in the Cave

Living in the Highlands

Long ago people in the Highlands lived in big families called clans. Every clan had a chief. He looked after his people and ruled them like a king. Each clan had its own district to stay in.

The chief rented some of his land to his brothers, sons and cousins. Some of them would be called lairds. The people of the clan gave hens' eggs or corn to their lairds to pay rent. All the people in the clan had the same surname.

Some clan names

Bruce	MacArthur	MacHugh
Campbell	McBride	McIan
Graham	MacDonald	Mackay
Grant	McEwan	McLean
Morrison	MacFarlane	MacMillan
Murray	McGregor	McRobert
Ogilvy		
Stewart		

Many clan names begin with Mac or Mc. This means "son of". MacDonald means "son of Donald".

People wore clothes made from a cloth called **tartan**. It had threads of many colours woven in a pattern of lines.

Often clans in the Highlands were at war with one another. They might fight about the border between their lands. Sometimes young men would steal sheep and cattle from another clan. If a man from one clan was killed by someone from another clan, his people might make war.

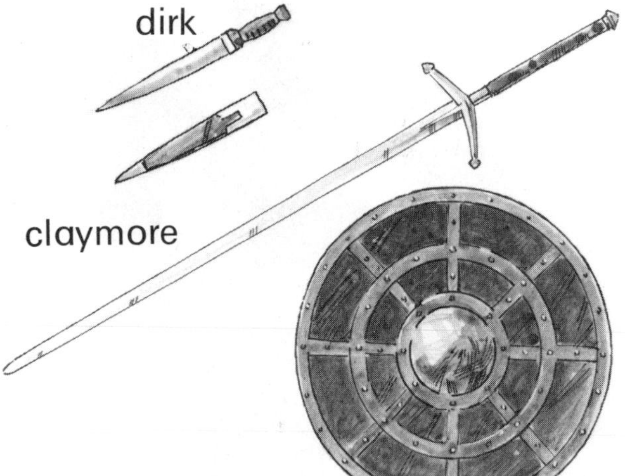

When the chief went to war, all the men of his clan had to fight too.

Men at war had a big sword called a **claymore** and a small dagger called a **dirk**.

The Blacksmith

The blacksmith who married Donald's nurse was a busy man. He made everything of metal that was needed for fighting. A blacksmith had to be very strong to swing a heavy hammer.

11. The Children with no Home

The great hall of Huntly Castle was full of people. Busy servants carried huge plates of food to the tables. The chief of clan Gordon was giving a feast.

Turning to his friend, the Laird of Grant, he said, "Now that you have eaten your fill, we have some fine sport for you to watch."

He led the way to a balcony above the kitchen. In the centre of the floor stood a large tub of the kind used for pig food. Servants were throwing all the left-over scraps into it. There were pieces of fat, half-chewed bones and crusts of bread.

"Perhaps this is for the dogs," thought the Laird of Grant.

Just then the cook took out a silver whistle. He blew two short blasts. A hatch on the wall was lifted up. In rushed a huge mob of children dressed in rags and tatters. They fought and scratched and bit each other to get at the food.

The noise was so great it might have been made by a pack of dogs.

"Ho, ho, ho!" laughed Huntly. "What do you think of that!"

The Laird of Grant did not laugh.

"Who are these poor young people?" he asked. He was shocked to hear that they were orphan children. He had helped to attack their clan the year before and their mothers and fathers had been killed. Now they had no one to care for them.

Grant felt he must try to help. Turning to Huntly he said, "You have kept them for a year and a day. Let me do the same."

He gave orders for the 200 boys and girls to be brought to Grant Castle. They were given a good meal and new clothes. Then he asked the people of his clan to take care of them. All the children were given the Grant name. Now they belonged to clan Grant. They had found a new home.

The Children with no Home

The Kitchen of Huntly Castle

When the chief of clan Gordon gave a feast, the servants in the castle kitchen were very busy. There were two huge fireplaces with great log fires. At one a boy cooked the meat. He turned the handle of a long spit.

The fat from the meat dripped into a pan. It was very hot beside the fire.

At the other a boy stood inside the fireplace. He turned the spits to roast geese, chickens and other birds.

The cook made meat pies and cooked them in the big brick ovens.

When all was ready the pages carried the food to the tables in the great hall.

Food

The men of the clans hunted deer and goats and game birds in the hills.

They caught fish. They kept herds of cattle.

Very often they had broth to eat.

Here is a dish which the men of the clans ate sometimes.

Haggis

Chop up onions, oatmeal and suet. Cut up the heart, lungs and liver of a sheep. Mix all together. Sew up in the lining of a sheep's stomach. Boil up for a long time.

12. Uproar in the Church

It was Sunday in Edinburgh, and a great crowd of people went to the church of St Giles. They wanted to see what would happen. King Charles I had ordered a new prayer book to be used in churches in Scotland. It set out the way in which people should worship. Many Scots did not like the new book. They thought it would make their church just like the church in England. They were angry with the king and his churchmen.

Many important people were in St Giles that day. Two archbishops dressed in rich robes led the way to the front. The Dean began to read from the prayer book. There was a loud rumble of noise from the crowd but no one moved. Sitting near the front was an old woman called Jenny Geddes. During the week she sold vegetables from a stall in the High Street.

"I'm not going to listen to this!" she cried.

She lifted the stool she had been sitting on and threw it at the Dean's head! At once other people joined in. The Dean's gown was torn from his back as he tried to move away. When the Bishop of Edinburgh went to the pulpit to speak, the crowd pelted him with rubbish.

A mob of people outside threw stones through the windows of the church. As fast as they could, the churchmen hurried off. No one was brave enough to read from the king's new book.

Jenny Geddes had caused an uproar in the church!

Uproar in the Church

The churches in Scotland and England were not the same. Even the ministers did not dress in the same way.

King Charles I was King of Scotland and King of England. He wanted the churches to be like one another.

He lived in England. So he did not know how angry the Scots would be when he tried to change their church.

The Church of Scotland Today

The Church of Scotland still is not the same as the church of England. Every year the special meeting of the church called the General Assembly meets in Edinburgh.

The Scottish word for a church is **kirk**. The Kirk of St Giles is in the Royal Mile in Edinburgh.

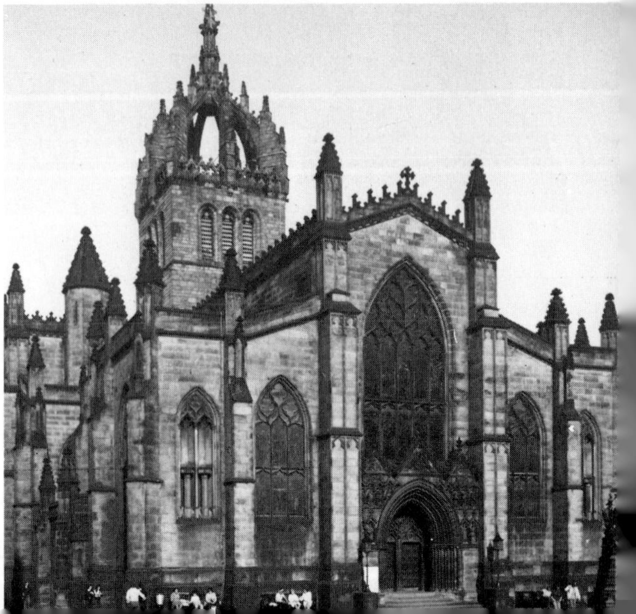

Churches Long Ago

Long ago when people went to church they had to stand. Some men sat on benches at the side. Older women sometimes had a stool to sit on.

Jenny Geddes's Shop

Jenny Geddes sold vegetables. Her shop was a stall set up in the street in front of her home. Shops like this were called **booths**.

Some shops had signs to show what they sold. What did the shops with these signs sell?

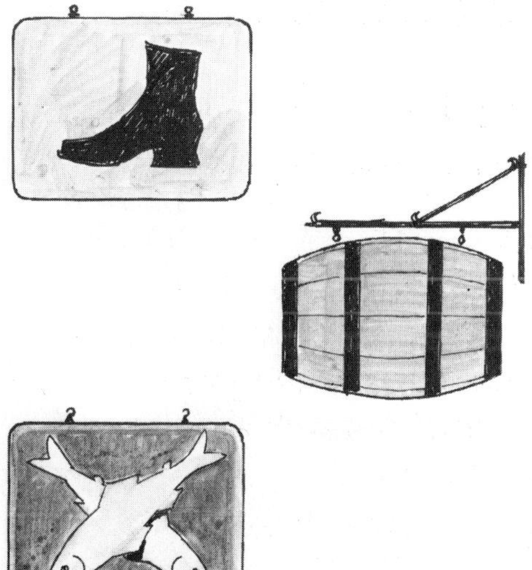

13. The Well-Fed Witches

In the town of Haddington nearly everyone was growing thin, pale and weak. Poor people begged for help from anyone who was a little better off. The harvest in Scotland had been bad and there was not enough food to eat. Many people were starving.

One old woman and her daughter never asked for help. As everyone else grew weaker for want of food, they stayed well and strong. They did not seem to have any extra food to eat. People said they must be witches, and they were put in prison.

One of the king's judges did not believe this. He went to see the two women in prison.

"Do not worry," he said. "I will not harm you. Tell me your secret. Why have you not gone hungry like everyone else?"

The old lady and her daughter whispered together. Then they said, "The secret is beneath an old trunk in the hut where we live. Push the trunk away and dig up the earth below."

The judge could not think what treasure might be hidden below the trunk. He hurried off to find out. When he had cleared away the earth, he found two jars. One was nearly empty. The other was full of salted snails! When food grew scarce, the two women had gathered snails and stored them. This was the secret of the well-fed witches!

The Well-Fed Witches

Long ago people thought that witches could do harm by working magic spells. Often the people called witches were just harmless old women who lived alone and had few friends. When things went wrong or something strange happened, witches were blamed. One old lady was put to death because she had argued with the people who lived next door. She was seen looking over the wall at her neighbour's cow. The cow died the next day and she was blamed.

Witch Fun

Not many people in Scotland nowadays think witches can harm them. Sometimes children dress up as witches at Hallowe'en. They pretend to work magic spells. Often someone acts as a witch in a Christmas pantomime. There are usually good and bad witches in fairy tales.

Eating Snails

Perhaps you would not like to eat snails unless you were very, very hungry. In some countries people think snails are very good to eat.

Here is a French recipe.

We eat what we are used to eating. People from other countries might not like our food.

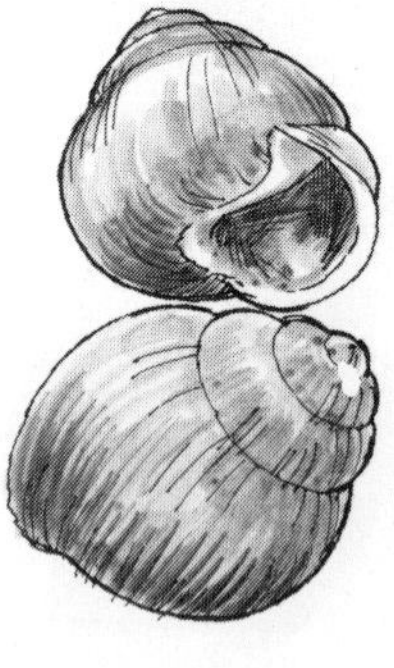

Cook snails in boiling water for three hours.
Add spices.
Strain off the water. Pull the snails out of their shells. Put the snails in a dish.
Mix salt, pepper, butter, parsley and nutmeg together.
Put this over the warm snails.

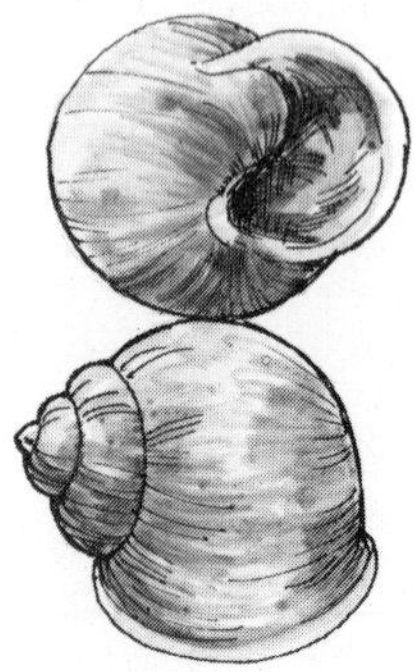

Charms

Long ago people had lucky charms or sayings to keep them from harm. Today people still do things to bring them good luck.

See how many of these things you do.

Cross your fingers
Touch wood
Have a lucky mascot
Blow out birthday candles with
  one puff
Think a black cat is lucky
Give a bride a silver horseshoe
Make a wish on a wishbone

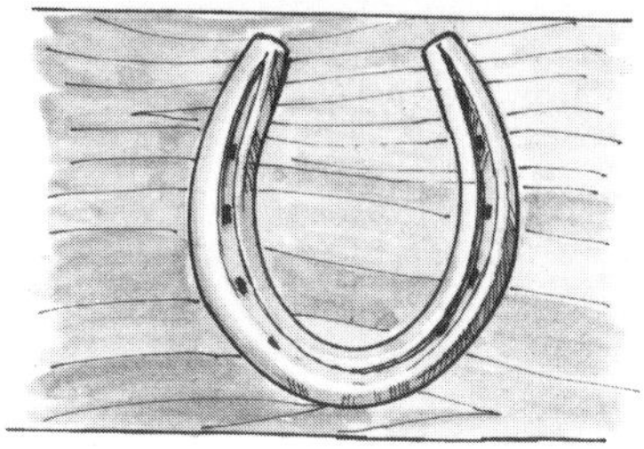

How many of these things would you try not to do?

Spill salt
Break a mirror
Walk under a ladder
Walk on cracks in the
  pavement
Put up an umbrella in the
  house
Choose 13 as a good number

Here are some magic sayings. Perhaps you know others.

Rain, rain go away
Come again some other day.

Eeksie, peeksie, hally go lum
Make a wish and it's sure to
  come.

14. Death in the Glen

The snow was falling heavily as the chief of the MacDonalds of Glencoe rode into Inverary. He looked very old and tired. For five days he had struggled through the snow. He must find the sheriff of Argyll and swear to obey the new King William.

"I wish I had not made a mistake and gone to Fort William," he thought. "Now I am late. It is past the time to make my promise to obey the new king."

The sheriff felt sorry for the old man.

"Do not worry," he said. "I will explain that you went to the wrong place to make your promise. Go home now. Everything will be all right. Your clan will not be harmed."

About a month later the people of Glencoe were surprised to see soldiers in the glen. They were led by Captain Campbell of Glenlyon.

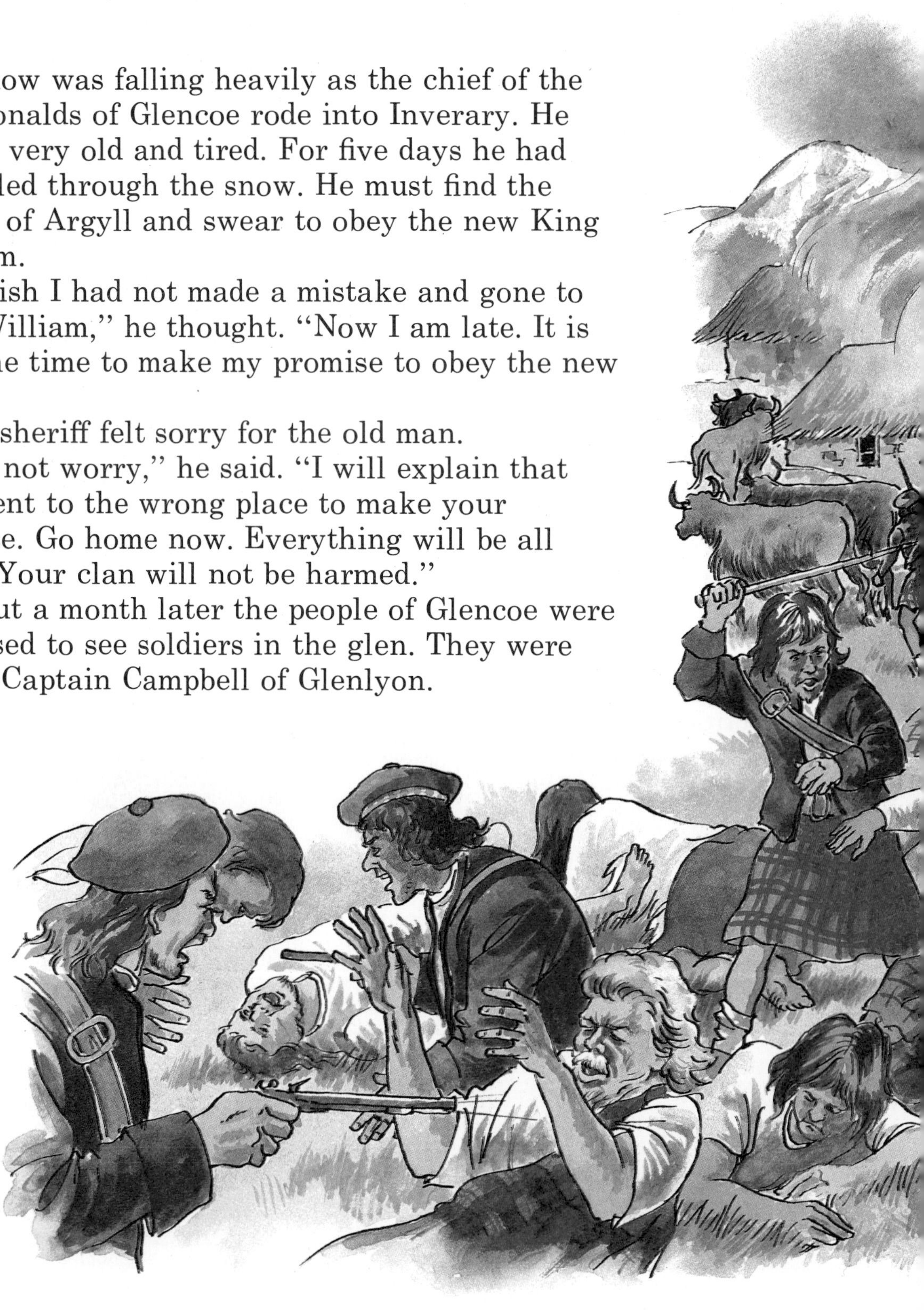

"We come as friends," he said smiling. "We wish to stay in the glen for a few days."

The people of the Highlands have always been very kind to visitors. The MacDonalds gave food and shelter to the Campbells and tried to make them feel welcome.

For two weeks the Campbells stayed in Glencoe. Then, early one morning, while the MacDonalds were sleeping, their visitors suddenly attacked. The chief was killed as he tried to get out of bed. Many people, old and young, were put to death. Those who escaped had to make their way through the deep snow on the high mountains around the glen.

As the winter sun rose, all was still and quiet. No cooking pots heated on the fire. No children played outside their houses. No women went about their work.

Death had come to the glen.

Death in the Glen

By the time of this story, nearly 300 years ago, Scotland and England had joined to make one country. Many nobles did not like King James Stewart. They asked William of Orange in Holland to rule instead with his wife Mary.

William brought an army and took over Britain. He worried that some Highland chiefs might still want James to be king. He asked everyone to make a promise to obey him.

When MacDonald of Glencoe came too late to make his promise, King William and his men were angry. They did not trust the MacDonalds. So they asked the Campbells to arrest the leaders. The Campbells were enemies of the MacDonalds. They made it an excuse to kill men, women and children.

Breaking the Custom

The people of the Highlands always gave visitors and strangers the best food and shelter they had. Once a person was made welcome and given food he could not be attacked. Even if he was found to be an enemy he would not be harmed. A Highland visitor would never hurt people he stayed with.

When the Campbells killed the MacDonalds of Glencoe, the news went all round Scotland. Everyone was shocked. They did not think Highland men would do such a thing.

15. Over the Sea to Skye

It was a warm June night. Early in the day Flora had brought her brother's cattle up the hill to feed on the summer grass. Now, as she lay resting in the hut, she thought she heard a noise. She lit a candle and looked round.

Flora's cousin stood by the door.

"We want you to help us, Flora," he said. "The prince is in danger."

"What can I do?" she asked.

Another man stepped forward.

"Come with me and meet the prince," he said.

Bonnie Prince Charlie did not look like a prince when Flora met him. He had no servants with him.

For weeks he had been hiding out in the hills. He bowed low and kissed Flora's hand.

"My friends have a plan," he said. "You are on a visit to your brother's house here in South Uist. Soon you will be going home to Skye. Will you take me with you? I want to get a ship at Portree. It will take me to France."

"But you will be captured," cried Flora.

"I shall travel as your servant," said the prince. "My name will be Betty Burke."

Flora knew there was great danger. If she was caught, she would be put in prison. Perhaps she might be killed. Yet she made up her mind to help the prince.

A few days later she brought the clothes to dress Prince Charles as a woman. There was a dress with purple flowers, a petticoat, a white cap and an apron. Charles laughed as he put them on. Flora told him he must try to walk like a lady and take smaller steps.

After a hard journey they set out for Skye with a few others in an open boat. The sea was wild and the rain fell heavily. The prince seemed happy and sang songs. When they landed at last there were armed men on the shore hunting for the prince.

"Who is this?" they asked roughly.

"This is my Irish maid," said Flora. "She does not speak any English!"

They were allowed to pass.

Flora MacDonald had helped the prince to escape once more from his enemies.

Over the Sea to Skye

Flora MacDonald knew that the enemies of Bonnie Prince Charlie were hunting him all over the Highlands. He had tried to win back Scotland for his father. Many Scots had fought for him. He had lost at the battle of Culloden. He must escape to France.

Anyone who told where Bonnie Prince Charlie was hiding would get a huge reward of £30,000. Most of the people who lived in the Highlands were very poor. Yet no one told his secret.

Charles was able to reach France. He never came back to Scotland. One song people used to sing about him was, "Will ye no' come back again?" Here is part of another song.

Speed bonnie boat like a bird on the wing
Over the sea the Skye
Carry the lad that is born to be king
Over the sea to Skye.

Punishing the Highlands

The people of the Highlands were punished because they helped the prince.

Some chiefs lost their lands. People were not allowed to have weapons.

A Highland man wore a kilt. He had a tartan plaid over his shoulder. For a long time after Charles went away no one in the Highlands could wear tartan.

Some families went to other lands across the sea. Flora MacDonald went to America. Some went to work in factories in the towns.

It was never the same again in the Highlands.

Index